HARRY N. ABRAMS, INC., PUBLISHERS, NEW YORK

LIBRARY OF CONGRESS CATALOGING IN PUBLICATION DATA
AVEDON, RICHARD.
IN THE AMERICAN WEST.
1. PHOTOGRAPHY—PORTRAITS. 2. WEST (U.S.)—BIOGRAPHY
—PORTRAITS. 1. TITLE.
TR680.A889   1985   779'.2'0924   84-28317
ISBN 0—8109—1105—1
ISBN 0—8109—2301—7 (PBK.)

PUBLISHED IN 1985 BY HARRY N. ABRAMS, INCORPORATED, NEW YORK
ALL RIGHTS RESERVED. NO PART OF THE CONTENTS OF THIS BOOK MAY BE
REPRODUCED WITHOUT THE WRITTEN PERMISSION OF THE PUBLISHERS

PRINTED AND BOUND IN JAPAN

THE AMON CARTER MUSEUM IN FORT WORTH, TEXAS, AND ITS DIRECTOR, MITCHELL A. WILDER, HAD BUILT A UNIQUE COLLECTION OF NINETEENTH- AND TWENTIETH-CENTURY PHOTOGRAPHS ON THE WEST. WILDER SAW A PORTRAIT OF WILBUR POWELL, A RANCH FOREMAN, WHICH WAS ONE OF A SERIES OF PHOTOGRAPHS I HAD TAKEN ON JULY 4, 1978, IN ENNIS, MONTANA. HE PROPOSED THAT I CONTINUE THIS WORK WITH THE SPONSORSHIP OF THE MUSEUM. WE AGREED THAT AN EXHIBITION WOULD BE COMPLETED IN FIVE SUMMERS, THAT IT WOULD OPEN AT THE AMON CARTER IN THE FALL OF 1985, AND THAT THE ORIGINAL NEGATIVES AND A SET OF PRINTS WOULD BECOME A PERMANENT PART OF THE MUSEUM'S ARCHIVES. WHEN WILDER DIED IN APRIL 1979, THE SUPPORT HE HAD GIVEN WAS CONTINUED BY THE STAFF OF THE MUSEUM.

R.A.

Allen Silvy, drifter
Route 93, Chloride, Nevada, 12/14/80

Loretta, Loudilla, and Kay Johnson, co-presidents, Loretta Lynn Fan Club
Wild Horse, Colorado, 6/16/83

Clifford Feldner, unemployed ranch hand
Golden, Colorado, 6/15/83

IN THE

AMERICAN

WEST

✦ ✦ ✦

1979–1984

Mary Watts, factory worker, and her niece Tricia Steward
Sweetwater, Texas, 3/10/79

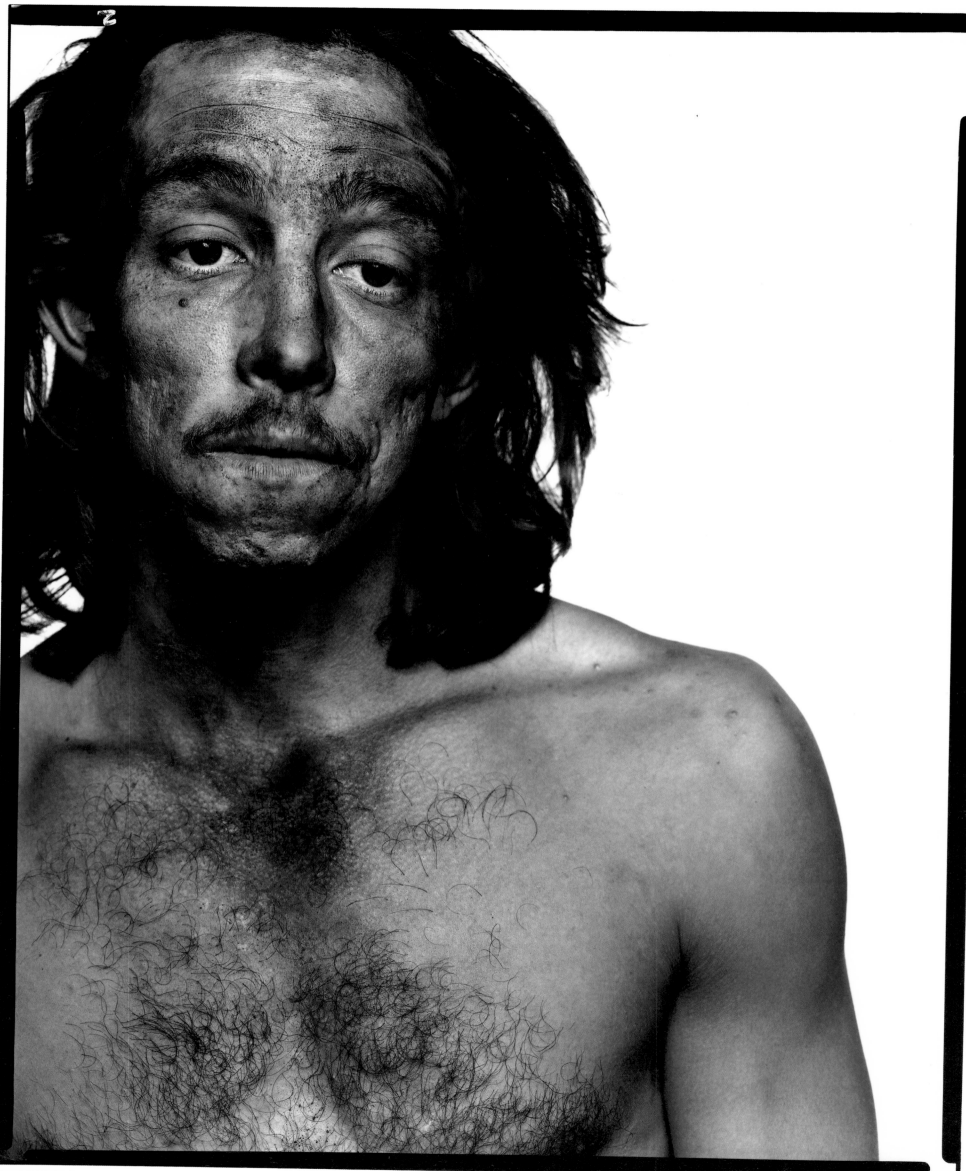

Hansel Nicholas Burum, coal miner
Somerset, Colorado, 12/17/79

RICHARD

AVEDON

✦ ✦

photographs

Benson James, drifter
Route 66, Gallup, New Mexico, 6/30/79

Patricia Wilde, housekeeper
Kalispell, Montana, 6/12/81

FOREWORD

Beginning in the spring of 1979 I spent the summer months traveling in the West, going to truck stops, stockyards, walking through the crowds at a fair, looking for faces I wanted to photograph. The structure of the project was clear to me almost from the start and each new portrait had to find its place in that structure. As the work progressed, the portraits themselves began to reveal connections of all kinds—psychological, sociological, physical, familial—among people who had never met.

This is how these portraits were made. I photograph my subject against a sheet of white paper about nine feet wide by seven feet long that is secured to a wall, a building, sometimes the side of a trailer. I work in the shade because sunshine creates shadows, highlights, accents on a surface that seem to tell you where to look. I want the source of light to be invisible so as to neutralize its role in the appearance of things.

I use an 8 x 10 view camera on a tripod, not unlike the camera used by Curtis, Brady, or Sander, except for the speed of the shutter and film. I stand next to the camera, not behind it, several inches to the left of the lens and about four feet from the subject. As I work I must imagine the pictures I am taking because, since I do not look through the lens, I never see precisely what the film records until the print is made. I am close enough to touch the subject and there is nothing between us except what happens as we observe one another during the making of the portrait. This exchange involves manipulations, submissions. Assumptions are reached and acted upon that could seldom be made with impunity in ordinary life.

Roy Gustavson, unemployed copper miner, and his wife, Judy, waitress
Butte, Montana, 7/1/83

A portrait photographer depends upon another person to complete his picture. The subject imagined, which in a sense is me, must be discovered in someone else willing to take part in a fiction he cannot possibly know about. My concerns are not his. We have separate ambitions for the image. His need to plead his case probably goes as deep as my need to plead mine, but the control is with me.

A portrait is not a likeness. The moment an emotion or fact is transformed into a photograph it is no longer a fact but an opinion. There is no such thing as inaccuracy in a photograph. All photographs are accurate. None of them is the truth.

The first part of the sitting is a learning process for the subject and for me. I have to decide upon the correct placement of the camera, its precise distance from the subject, the distribution of the space around the figure, and the height of the lens. At the same time, I am observing how he moves, reacts, expressions that cross his face so that, in making the portrait, I can heighten through instruction what he does naturally, how he is.

The subject must become familiar with the fact that, during the sitting, he cannot shift his weight, can hardly move at all, without going out of focus or changing his position in the space. He has to learn to relate to me and the lens as if we were one and the same and to accept the degree of discipline and concentration involved. As the sitting goes on, he begins to understand what I am responding to in him and finds his own way of dealing with that knowledge. The process has a rhythm that is punctuated by the click of the shutter and my assistants changing the plates of film after each exposure. There are times when I speak and times when I do not, times when I react too strongly and destroy the tension that is the photograph.

These disciplines, these strategies, this silent theater, attempt to achieve an illusion: that everything embodied in the photograph simply happened, that the person in the portrait was always there, was never told to stand there, was never encouraged to hide his hands, and in the end was not even in the presence of a photographer.

Richard Avedon

Vivian Richardson and her granddaughter Heidi Zacher
Deadwood, South Dakota, 8/6/82

65

Bill Curry, drifter
Interstate 40, Yukon, Oklahoma, 6/16/80

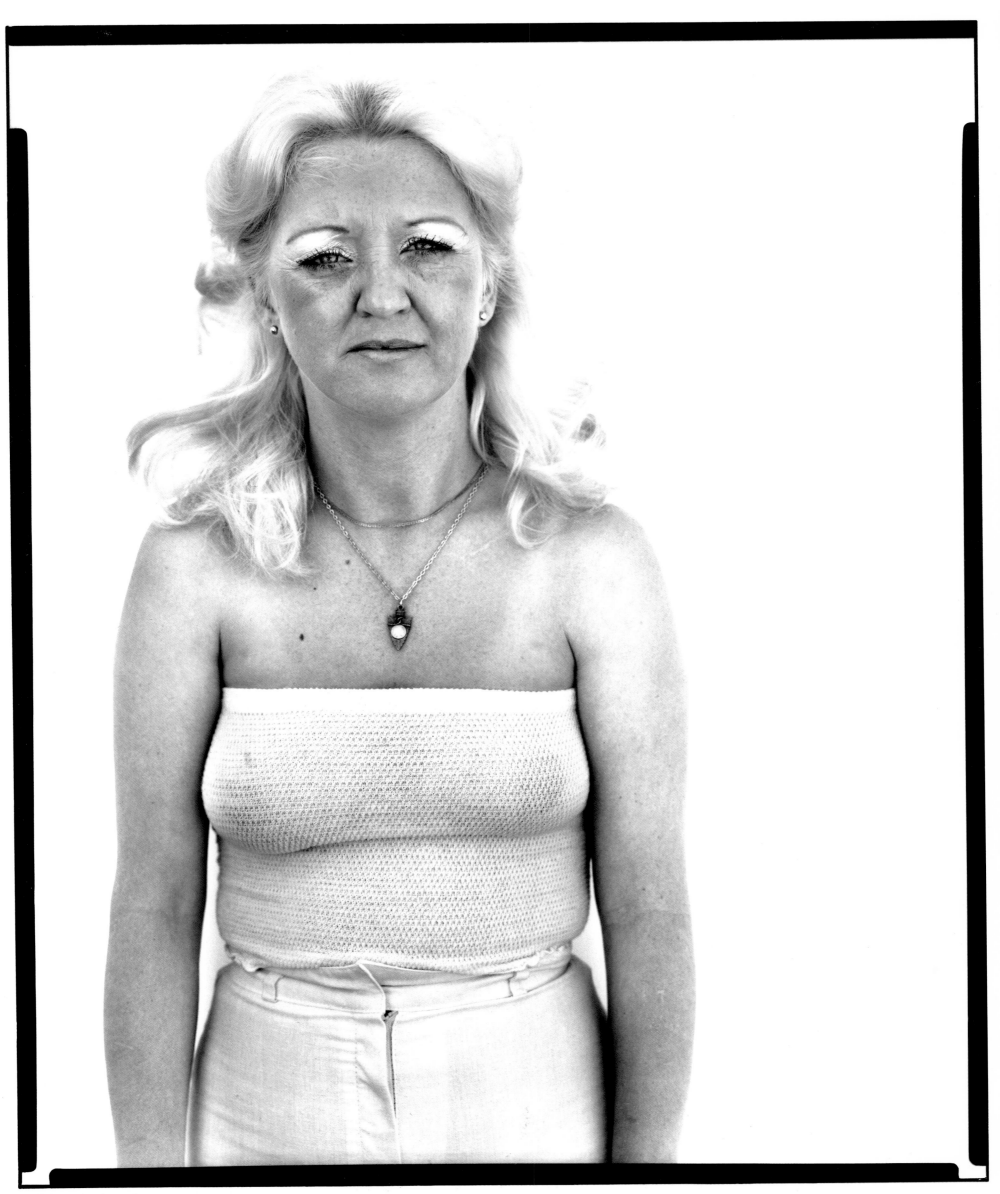

Carol Crittendon, bartender
Butte, Montana, 7/1/81

Lyal Burr, coal miner, and his sons Kerry and Phillip
The Church of Jesus Christ of Latter-Day Saints, Koosharem, Utah, 5/7/81

James Lykins, oil field worker
Rawson, North Dakota, 8/17/82

Sandra Bennett, twelve year old
Rocky Ford, Colorado, 8/23/80

Debbie McClendon, carney
Thermopolis, Wyoming, 7/29/81

Rusty McCrickard, janitor, Tracey Featherston, motel maid
Dixon, California, 5/10/81

Richard Wheatcroft, rancher
Jordan, Montana, 6/19/81 and 6/27/83

Robert Dixon, meat packer
Aurora, Colorado, 6/15/83

Della Trujillo, waitress
Santuario de Chimayo, New Mexico, Good Friday, 4/4/80

James Kimberlin, drifter
State Road 18, Hobbs, New Mexico, 10/7/80

Juan Patricio Lobato, carney
Rocky Ford, Colorado, 8/23/80

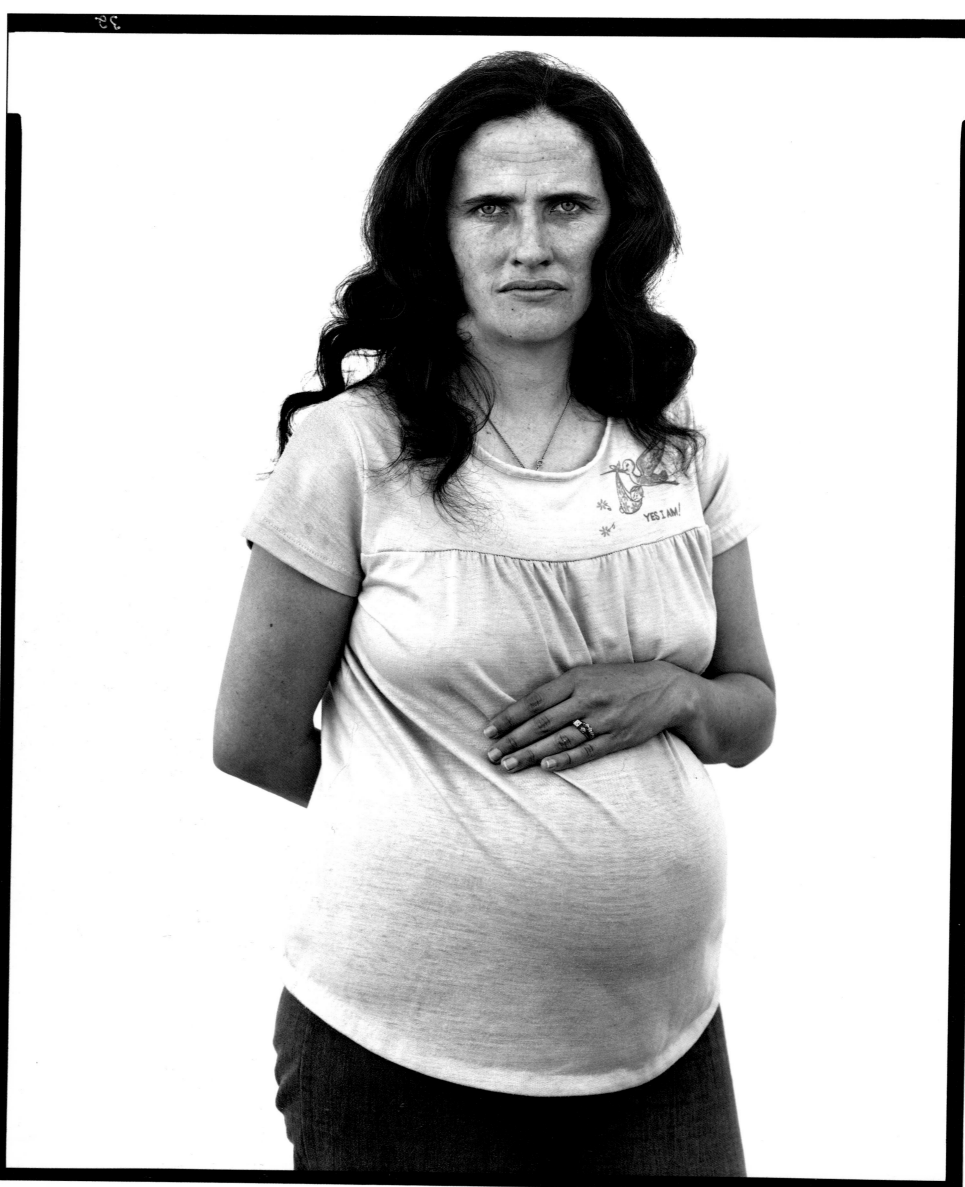

Emma Lee Wellington, housewife
North Las Vegas, Nevada, 12/15/80

Unidentified migrant worker
Eagle Pass, Texas, 12/10/79

David Beason, shipping clerk
Denver, Colorado, 7/25/81

Shawna Callahan, thirteen year old
Cheyenne, Wyoming, 7/30/82

Rocky Burch, fifteen year old
Burley, Idaho, 8/19/83

Jay Greene, grain thresher
Burley, Idaho, 8/19/83

Annette Gonzales, housewife, and her sister Lydia Ranck, secretary
Santuario de Chimayo, New Mexico, Easter Sunday, 4/6/80

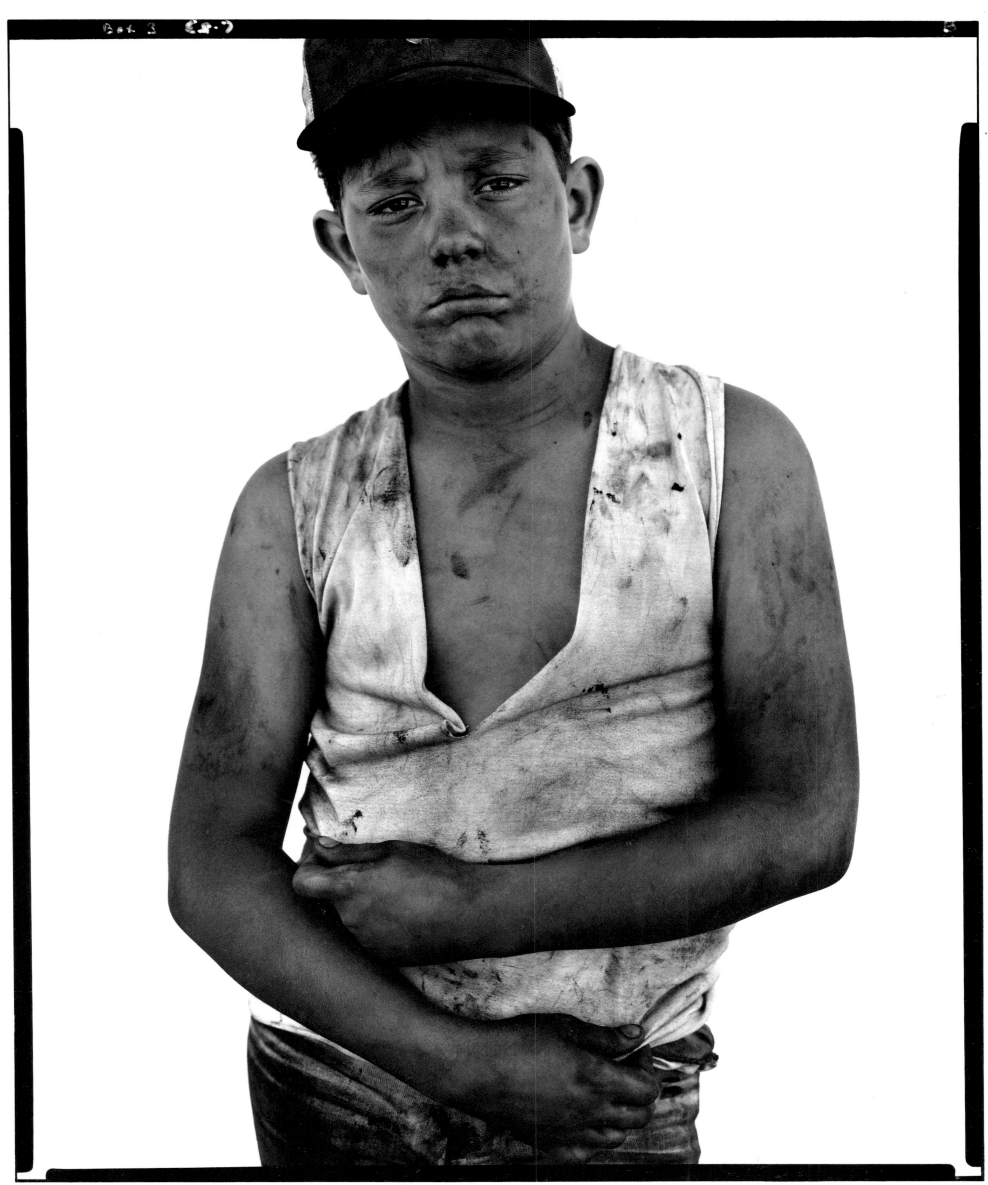

Bubba Morrison, oil field worker
Albany, Texas, 6/10/79

Milo DeWitt, cowboy
Payson, Arizona, 8/29/82

Charlene Van Tighem, physical therapist
Augusta, Montana, 6/26/83

Dawn Jaynes, waitress, Clint Jones, ranch hand
Rocky Ford, Colorado, 8/23/80

G.R. Cook III, rodeo contestant
Douglas, Wyoming, 7/27/81

Leonard Ray Blanchard, ex-prize fighter
Las Vegas, Nevada, 12/14/80

Mike Bencich, Dan Ashberger, coal miners
Somerset, Colorado, 8/29/80

B.J. Van Fleet, nine year old
Ennis, Montana, 7/2/82

Clarence Lippard, drifter
Interstate 80, Sparks, Nevada, 8/29/83

Alfred Lester, dryland farmer
Charboneau, North Dakota, 8/17/82

Stan Riley, James Law, oil field workers
Albany, Texas, 6/10/79

Marie Larsen, patient
State Hospital, Las Vegas, New Mexico, 4/1/80

Tom Stroud, oil field worker
Velma, Oklahoma, 6/12/80

Rochelle Justin, patient
State Hospital, Las Vegas, New Mexico, 4/1/80

Carl Hoefert, unemployed blackjack dealer
Reno, Nevada, 8/30/83

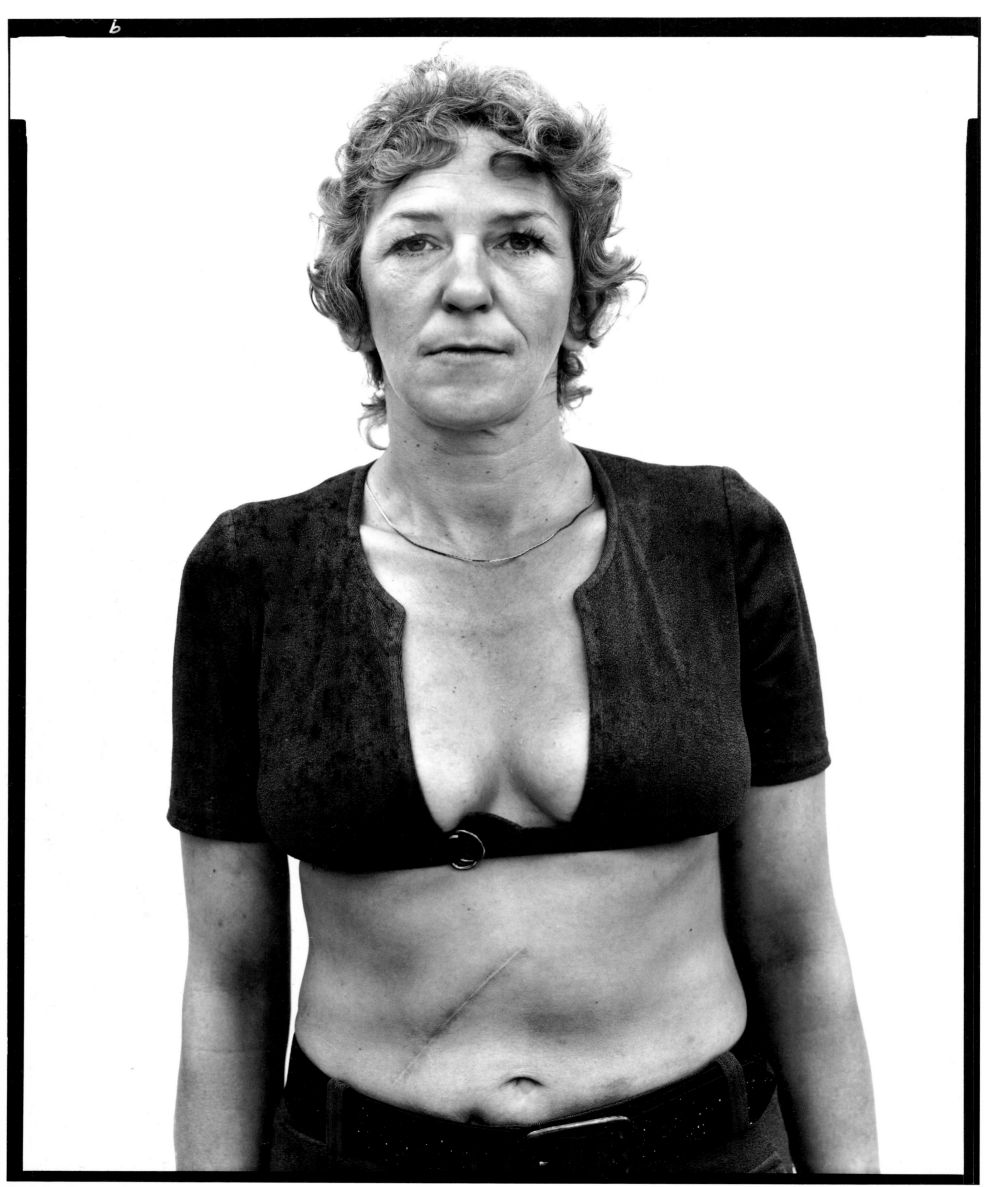

Beverly Jane Frazier, truck driver
Burley, Idaho, 8/20/83

Marvin Morrison, hay hauler, Kellie Bennett, salesgirl
Burley, Idaho, 8/19/83

Emory J. Stovall, scientist
Los Alamos, New Mexico, 6/12/79

Ann Marie Gustin, equipment specialist, USAF
Fort Bridger, Wyoming, 9/2/83

Billy Mudd, trucker
Alto, Texas, 5/7/81

Rita Carl, law enforcement student
Sweetwater, Texas, 3/10/79

John Harrison, lumber salesman, and his daughter Melissa
Lewisville, Texas, 11/22/81

Jonathan Stahl, blacksmith, Sam Stahl, farmer
Hutterite Colony, Gilford, Montana, 7/19/83

Jesse Kleinsasser, pig man
Hutterite Colony, Harlowton, Montana, 6/23/83

Mart Kleinsasser, sheep man, Mike Kleinsasser, cow man
Hutterite Colony, Harlowton, Montana, 6/23/83

David Wurtz, cemetery man
Hutterite Colony, Chester, Montana, 7/21/83

Eli Walter, Jr., chicken man
Hutterite Colony, Stanford, Montana, 7/23/83

James Story, coal miner
Somerset, Colorado, 12/18/79

Rick Davis, drifter
Interstate 94, Buffalo, North Dakota, 7/13/82

Blue Cloud Wright, slaughterhouse worker
Omaha, Nebraska, 8/10/79

Jesus Cervantes, Manuel Heredia, prisoners
Bexar County Jail, San Antonio, Texas, 6/5/80

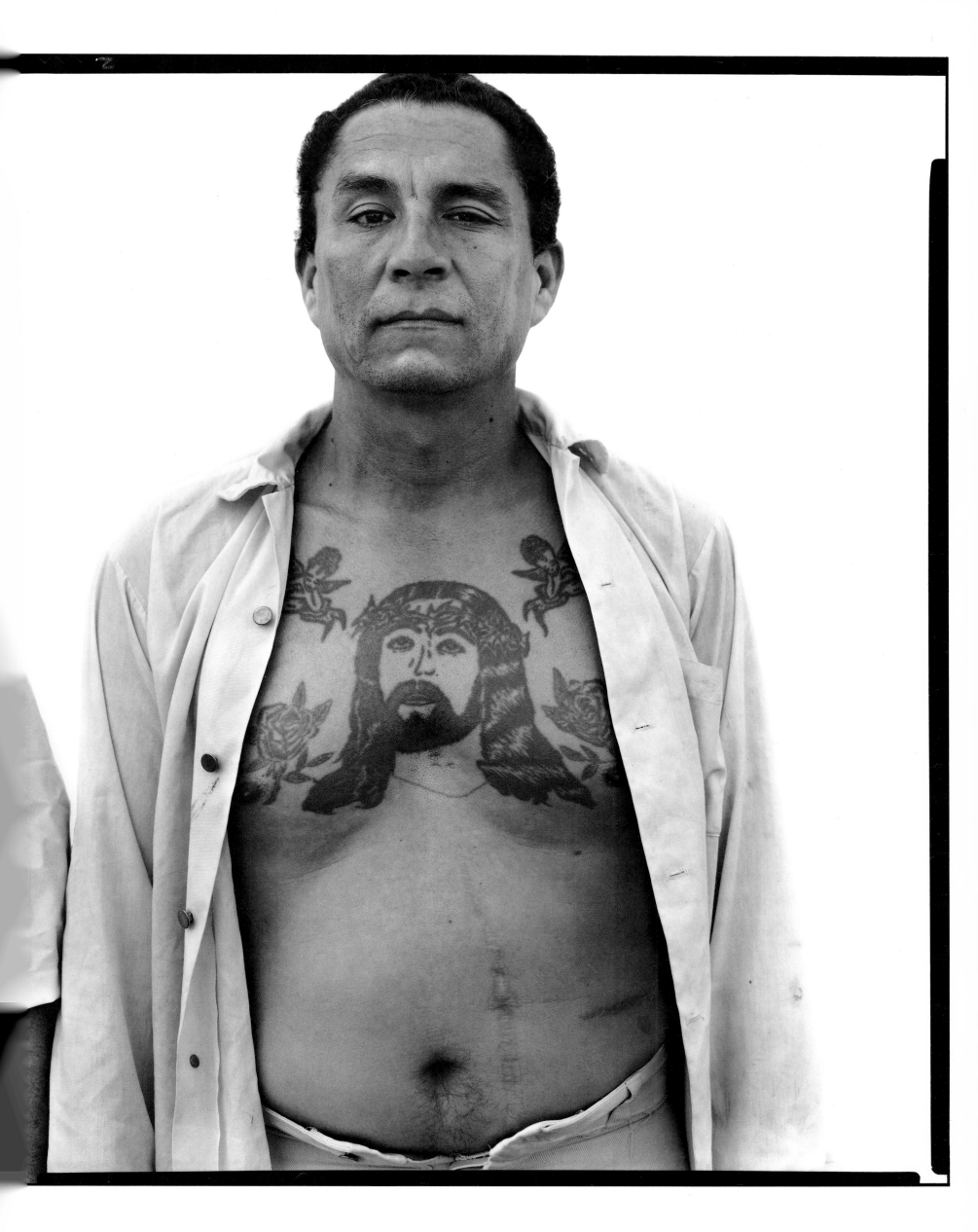

Roberto Lopez, oil field worker
Lyons, Texas, 9/28/80

Craig Panike, drummer
High School Band, Weiser, Idaho, 6/27/81

Reverend Andrew Goodwin, pastor
Baptist Church, Miles City, Montana, 5/18/81

Ruby Mercer, publicist
Frontier Days, Cheyenne, Wyoming, 7/31/82

Billy Joe Danos, day laborer
Cheyenne, Wyoming, 7/25/82

Jeannie Banta, waitress
Salmon, Idaho, 8/25/83

Bill Hanken, construction worker
Cody, Wyoming, 7/4/82

Danny Lane, fourteen year old, Christine Coil, seventeen year old
Calhan, Colorado, 7/31/81

Daniel Salozar, farmer
Santuario de Chimayo, New Mexico, Good Friday, 4/4/80

Teresa Waldron, fourteen year old, Joe College, rodeo contestant
Sidney, Iowa, 8/11/79

A.L. Bean, cotton farmer
Sweetwater, Texas, 3/10/79

Peggy Daniels, cashier
Giddings, Texas, 5/7/81

Russell Laird, Tammy Baker, seventeen year olds
Sweetwater, Texas, 3/10/79

Andrea D'Amato, student
Santa Fe, New Mexico, 4/3/80

Harrison Tsosie, cowboy
Navajo Reservation, Window Rock, Arizona, 6/13/79

Myrna Sandoval, eighteen year old, and her sister Claudia, fourteen year old
El Paso, Texas, 4/20/82

Petra Alvarado, factory worker
El Paso, Texas, on her birthday, 4/22/82

Robert Gonzalez, prisoner
Bexar County Jail, San Antonio, Texas, 6/5/80

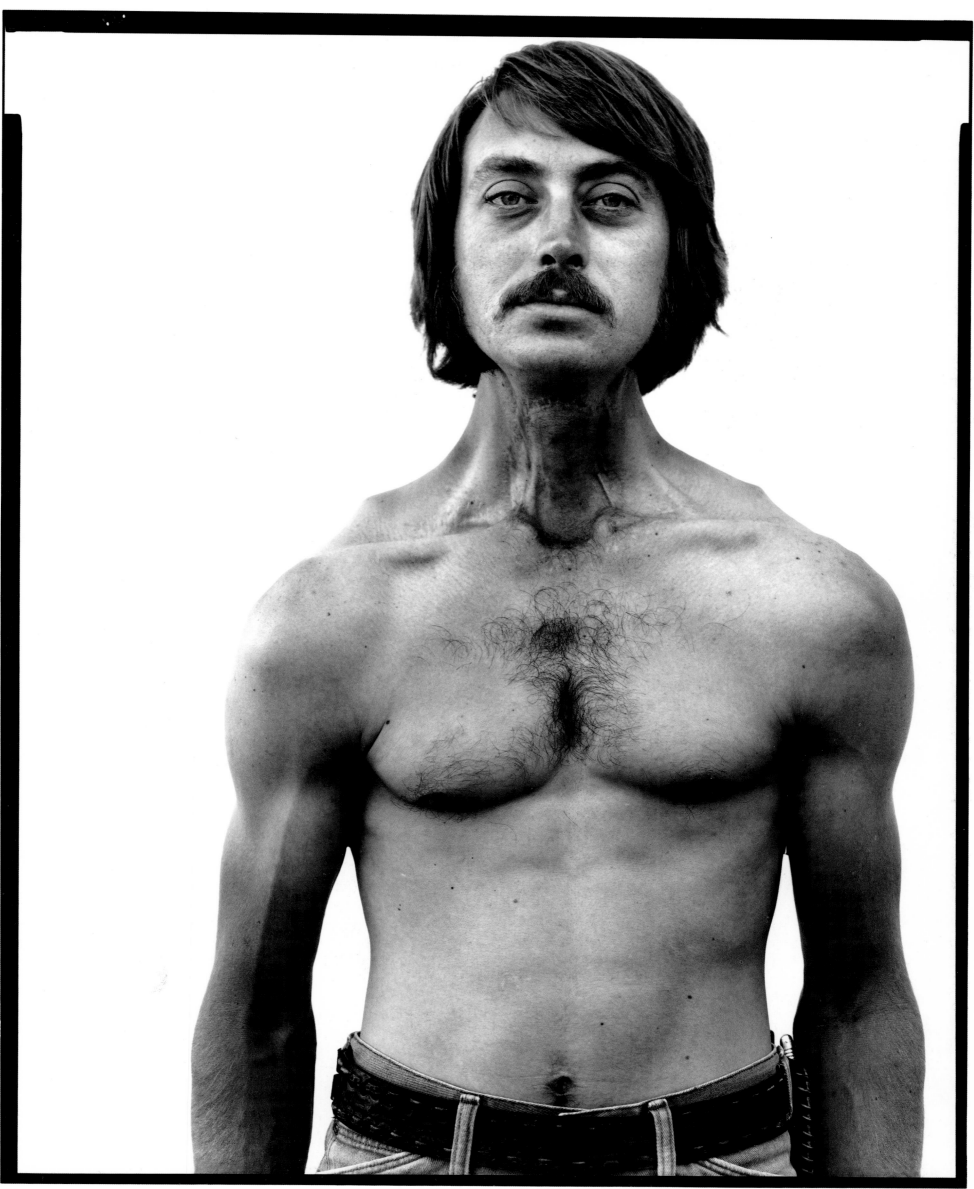

Dave Timothey, nuclear fallout victim
Orem, Utah, 8/8/80

Valentino Curley, grave digger
Navajo Reservation, Ganado, Arizona, 12/6/80

Gloria Cloud, waitress
Hobbs, New Mexico, 9/27/80

Lloyd Bloom, oil field worker
Williston, North Dakota, 8/21/82

Roy Honeycutt, rodeo stock contractor
Alamosa, Texas, 6/13/83

Gilbert Saavedra, patient
State Hospital, Las Vegas, New Mexico, 4/1/80

Steer
Slaughterhouse, Amarillo, Texas, 11/19/81

Joe Butler, coal miner
Reliance, Wyoming, 8/28/79

Ruby Holden, pawnbroker
Henderson, Nevada, 12/17/80

Sheep
Slaughterhouse, Ennis, Montana, 6/30/83

Debbie McIntyre, practical nurse, and her daughter Marie
Cortez, Colorado, 6/11/83

Richard Garber, drifter
Interstate 15, Provo, Utah, 8/20/80

Jimmy Lopez, gypsum miner
Sweetwater, Texas, 6/15/79

Steer
Slaughterhouse, Omaha, Nebraska, 8/10/79

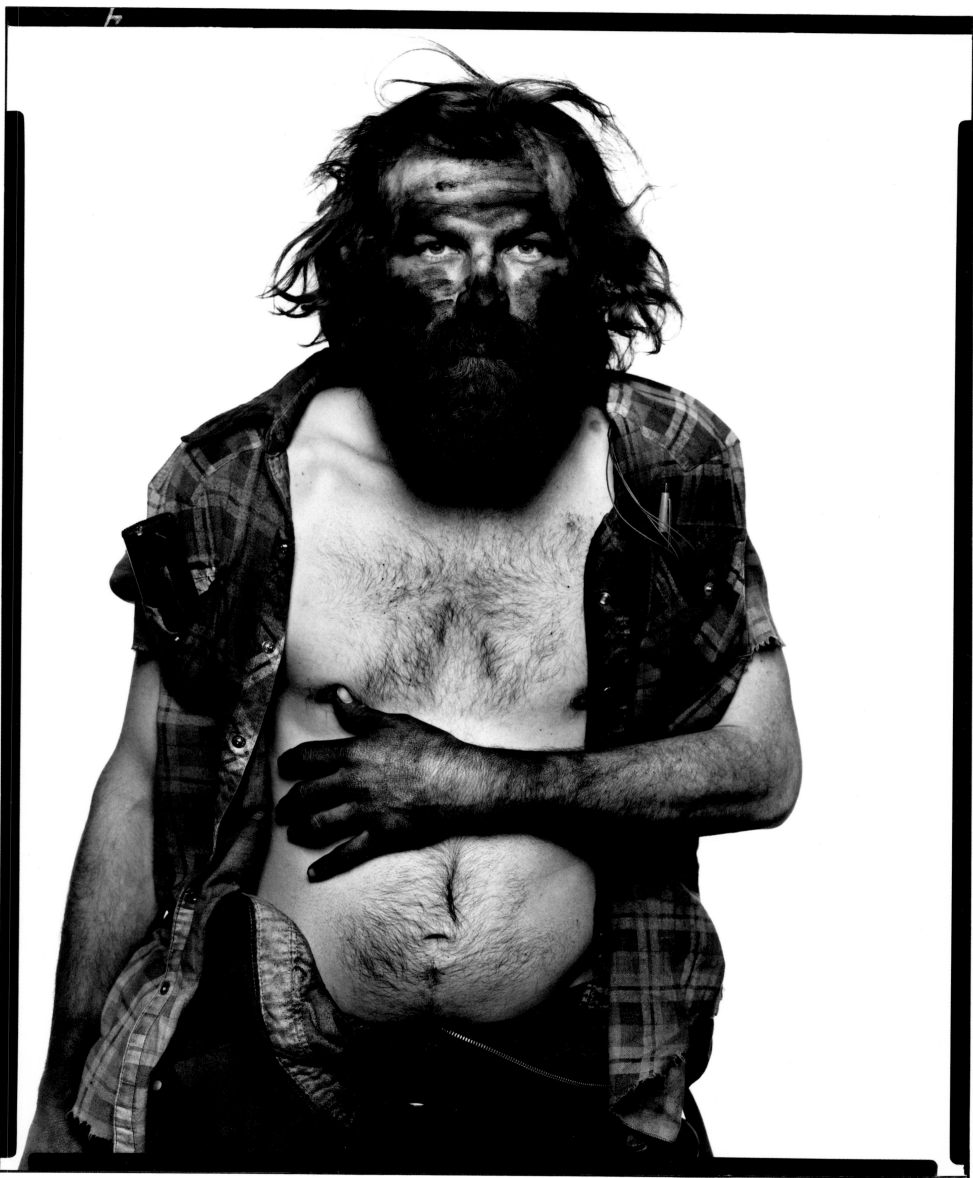

Edward Roop, coal miner
Paonia, Colorado, 12/19/79

Roger Skaarland, Jim Bingham, coal miners
Reliance, Wyoming, 8/29/79

Lance Barron, Mel Pyeatt, coal miners
Reliance, Wyoming, 8/28/79

Donald Keen, coal miner
Reliance, Wyoming, 8/28/79

Homer Emmons, coal miner
Somerset, Colorado, 8/28/80

Doug Harper, coal miner
Somerset, Colorado, 8/29/80

Roger Tims, Jim Duncan, Leonard Markley, Don Belak, coal miners
Reliance, Wyoming, 8/29/79

oil field worker
oma, 6/12/80

Boyd Fortin, thirteen year old
Sweetwater, Texas, 3/10/79

BACKGROUND

In the Callahan Divide country of West Texas, extensive gypsum formations give the creek water a bitter taste. One exception is a stream with its headwaters situated in the highest lands of Nolan County, named "mobeeti"—sweet water—by the Kiowa. In 1879, the stream drew some of the first white settlers to the area, and kept them there. They in turn named their town after it—Sweetwater.

Like most towns in the West, Sweetwater began to grow in earnest with the building of the railroads. In 1881, the Texas and Pacific extended tracks from Forth Worth through Abilene to Sweetwater, and from that time the town became a center for ranching and farming. Later, oil and gas production would overshadow the economic, but not symbolic, importance of ranching. Today, the people of Sweetwater manufacture goods ranging from gypsum products to radiation-detection equipment.

Each March for the past twenty-six years, the Jaycees of Sweetwater have sponsored a Rattlesnake Round-Up for the people of Nolan and the surrounding counties. The Round-Up is an attempt to rid the rangeland of snakes and make it safer for raising livestock, and most years around seven thousand pounds of rattlesnakes are brought into the Nolan County Coliseum, live. The Jaycees pay four dollars a pound for every snake. Farmers and ranchers, oil field roustabouts, railroad clerks, and kids all comb the countryside using large cylinders of pressurized gas to flush out snakes from their dens in the rock ledges.

There is no market for a dead snake. The meat spoils and it is hard to skin. The hunters bring them in alive in plastic trash cans and gunny sacks. There is a cash prize for longest; the heaviest is no longer a category because in the past some hunters poured buckshot down the gullets of their entries before a weigh-in. Handlers milk the snakes of their venom for medical research. The Jaycees Wives Club cut them up and deep fry them; others make the skins and carcasses into curios—paperweights, earrings, and beer mugs. Friday night, Miss Snake Charmer is chosen from the senior class of Sweetwater High School, and Saturday night there is a Rattlesnake Dance.

Avedon came to this three-day event in the spring of 1979. He worked with two assistants. They set up a simple open-air studio by taping a large sheet of white seamless paper to an exterior wall of the Coliseum. The camera was a Deardorf, a large, cumbersome piece of equipment similar to the cameras used by portrait photographers a century ago. With this camera, the photographer stands under a black cloth to focus. The subject appears upside down and backwards on the ground glass. The process is time consuming. But Avedon's two assistants—one at the rear of the camera loading 8 x 10-inch sheets of film, the other up front at the lens, checking the aperture—allow him to work with surprising speed. Sometimes he photographs as quickly as if he were using a 35mm camera.

That March weekend, Avedon stood a young boy in front of the white paper. He had found him inside the Coliseum helping his father skin and gut rattlesnakes. Avedon photographed him in three sessions over two days. The portrait of Boyd Fortin, rattlesnake skinner, began the Western Project.

Right from the start, Avedon chose men and women who work at hard, uncelebrated jobs, the people who are often ignored or overlooked. He searched for what he wanted to see and his choices were completely subjective. In the tradition of itinerant Colonial portrait painters and nineteenth-century photographers of the frontier, Avedon explored hometowns and country fairs, rodeos and threshing bees, mining camps and drilling sites. He worked in the Great Plains and the Rocky Mountain states, going as far west as the Sierra Nevadas, as far north as Calgary, Canada, and south to the Mexican border. "This is a fictional West," Avedon has said. "I don't think the West of these portraits is any more conclusive than the West of John Wayne."

That weekend in Sweetwater was the first time I worked on the Western Project. I had been hired by Avedon and the Amon Carter Museum to do the research for the project and to help uncover photographic possibilities. One of the things we learned in Sweetwater was the importance of going to events that attracted large numbers of people. With the exception of urban areas, the West is sparsely populated. There are fewer than 480,000 people in the entire state of Wyoming. In the town of New England, North Dakota, six men plant and harvest thirteen thousand acres of sunflowers. Nearly all of Nevada is owned by the federal government, and so is the bulk of Utah, Idaho, and Oregon. These states may be rich in minerals, lumber, and livestock, but they are essentially empty of people.

We needed help in locating our subjects. A bucking-stock contractor told us we could find "the wildest one-day rodeo in America" in Augusta, Montana. A woman electrician we sat next to on a plane told us of a mine superintendent in Paonia, Colorado, who was known across the state as "Mr. Coal." Marta Weigle, a folklorist, was particularly generous in sharing her knowledge of New Mexico and the Penitentes. She made it possible for Avedon to photograph in the Sangre de Cristo mountain villages during Holy Week.

In Montana, we were helped by Doc and Olive Losee. They had settled in the Madison Valley in 1949 after he graduated from Yale Medical School. Olive is a registered nurse, and together they have spent their lives doctoring the people of Montana. They know their territory, and they pointed us to Butte.

✻ ✻ ✻

In its heyday, Butte, Montana, sat on top of "the richest hill on earth." Thousands of tunnels burrowed into the hillside. There were more miles of underground passageways in the Butte hill, so the saying goes, than there were miles of streets in New York City. Fifty-car ore trains left Butte loaded with copper and by-product metals every hour. In the years after World War II, Butte had six thousand miners underground: Italians, Finns, Slavs, and the descendants of the Irish and Cornish immigrants who had come to work in the mines of the 1880s. "The nightlife was fantastic," remembers Carl Rohan, cafe owner. "Why, down in Meaderville, at two o'clock in the morning, the street was so crowded you couldn't even wiggle."

The Berkley Pit opened in 1955. Mining engineers dug a hole in the hill that eventually became a mile and a half wide and more than a thousand feet deep. Victorian houses built by the first miners and outlined in gingerbread fretwork quivered on the edge of the pit. Each year, as the hole increased in size, more and more earth gave way. "So much has come and gone," said one miner. "The pit ate up the little town of McQueen where I was a kid."

When we first came to Butte, in 1979, it was still a one-company mining town, owned and operated by Anaconda since 1906. The Berkley Pit was in operation twenty-four hours a day. The copper industry itself, however, was beginning to show signs of depression. Butte's young men were no longer following their fathers' footsteps into the hill, and the only underground mine still in operation was the Kelly. Its safety engineer, Hugh Graham, took us through the main entrance and along a 390-foot tunnel leading to the shaft. "See this tunnel?" he said. "This section's been painted about two years. The walls are bare. You can always tell when the miners are old. There's no graffiti on the walls. If we had young miners, this tunnel would be covered."

As the day shift ended at the Kelly mine, the "cage," a two-deck elevator platform, brought seventy men up after eight hours underground. A miner told us he'd been down a mile. "None of us hears right," the miner said. "I can hear a group of men talking, but I can't tell one from the other. We drill with jack-legs, two in a small space. We're all deaf."

When we returned to Butte in 1980 and 1982, conditions had worsened. Butte was suffering from boomtown aftershock. The value of copper had dropped; it was now selling for seventy-five cents a pound. Yet it cost a dollar a pound to get out of the ground, and even then the ore was low-grade. The mine could not operate at a profit. Eighteen hundred miners were laid off. Seven hundred houses were for sale. The huge Berkley Pit was shut down. "Butte couldn't be worse if a cyclone hit it," said one miner. The big mining days were over. Now the Chamber of Commerce was trying to diversify the town's economic base. They wanted to attract new business—national franchises like Baskin-Robbins and Kentucky Fried Chicken.

Not far from Butte, isolated on large tracts of land and removed from the mainstream of American life, is a self-contained group of people called Hutterites. A conservative religious sect, the Hutterites originally fled persecution in Germany and came to the United States in the latter part of the nineteenth century. Today, Hutterite families live together in colonies of thirty-five to ninety people in central Montana and in Canada. They sustain themselves through hard work and the equal sharing of all profits and property. They shun most aspects of American life, preferring to avoid "those things which disrupt families." They do not send their children to public schools. They educate them at home to satisfy state laws, but the education is both limited and brief. They read the Bible. Televisions, radios, movies, even musical instruments are forbidden. And, although they follow the latest agricultural trends and use highly automated farm equipment, there is nothing so frivolous as a snowmobile or a dirt bike on a Hutterite farm.

Hutterites marry other Hutterites. There are four or five family names common to most colonies: Stahl, Kleinsasser, Waldner, and Wipf. Pragmatic and attentive to the doctrines of their religion, the Hutterites have maintained a remarkably strong identity. They are not losing their children to the cities. At a time when farms all over America are going under, the Hutterite farms are vigorous and prospering.

Every Hutterite works. The men raise livestock, plant crops, mend farm equipment. The women cook, clean, wash, and sew, and paint the colony's buildings. We saw small boys sorting eggs, herding cattle, driving tractors. Young girls help wash and clean and pick garden vegetables. Each person is connected to the land and dependent upon the weather. One afternoon as we visited a Hutterite family, a thunderstorm began to pile up. Through the window a sharp strip of lightning, brilliant against the dark sky, struck in a wheat field. The entire family rushed to the window. They knew that hail could wipe out a year's work in half an hour.

At the end of a day, when we were packing up our photographic equipment and talking to some Hutterite men, a girl whispered to us, "Mother says for you to come to our house." Four or five Hutterite children trailed us into the house. They had been bound to us at the start of the day by the miracle of the Polaroid. The mother and five daughters quickly drew up chairs for us. The portly grandfather, standing aside, one lifeless eye askew, nodded approvingly. The father came in, hot from the fields, his face and arms burned rust-red. Two favorite uncles entered. And from the doorway of his house, the Minister, who is the colony's boss, watched, not approving, but tolerating. The two uncles looked like twins, stout and strong, each with a shock of black hair matted by a cap to pale foreheads. One uncle, the "Cow Boss," began to sing quietly, tentatively. The other brother, dressed alike in homemade shirt and pants, pulled a small, secret harmonica from his pocket. Their voices became more assured as they sang verse after verse of Country-Western songs—songs like "Your Cheatin' Heart" and "I'm So Lonesome I Could Cry."

Several months later we returned to this colony. A woman told us that eleven days after we had left, her husband, the "Hog Boss," and his nephew were cleaning one of the pits in the pig barn. The barns are big, and the 250 animals stand on metal grates. The manure falls through to the pits below, which are cleaned out periodically. On that Saturday morning, the nephew was in a pit scraping down the waste while the uncle was watching from above. The nephew remembered his uncle talking. Then the uncle's voice seemed to fade away. That was when gas fumes from the manure knocked the young man unconscious. The uncle jumped into the pit to hoist up his nephew, but he, too, was overcome by the fumes. A short time later, two small boys wandered into the barn. Seeing the nephew sitting dazed by the front door, they ran for help. Two men came, understood immediately that the uncle was missing, and began to search the pits. One grate was still raised up. One of the men looked down into darkness but couldn't see. He reached his hand into the pit and felt the hogman. They gathered the uncle into their arms and carried him outside. He never regained consciousness. His wife wrote later, "His thirty-two years of very hard work were done. We can't put a question mark when the Lord had put a period. Paul never disgraced the Lord, nor His comments."

✧ ✧ ✧

We did not see Indians that looked like the ones in the portraits by Edward Curtis—steadfast, noble, and unbroken. The Navajo, Ute, Apache, and Crow tribes all have severe problems with alcoholism. Nobody, it seems, knows quite why. Some attribute the problem to reservation life itself—the isolation, lack of jobs, broken homes, and dependence on welfare. Indian women tend to drink as much as men. To many Indians with whom we spoke, the possibility of success in contemporary America seems remote. The grim testimony to the failure of the federal government's Indian policies is on record at the reservations we visited.

Driving south on Route 73, just beyond Whiteriver, Arizona, on the White Mountain Apache Reservation, we came across a convenience store that sells, among other things, high-proof wine—M. D. 20-20 and Thunderbird, mostly. The store used to sit just a few feet from Route 73. Some Apaches would come there to buy their liquor and begin drinkng as soon as they got outside. Drunk, they would wander around the building. More than one had stumbled to his death in the path of a pickup. The reservation authorities' solution to this problem was to move the store ninety-seven feet back from the highway on open land among buckbrush and native grasses.

On this cold December day, Indians were clustered outside the store in groups of two or three. Some stood out in the brush over an open fire, talking in drunken, rambling conversation; others leaned up against the wall, out of the December wind, on the sunny side of the building, passing around a bottle of Gypsy Rose. A disheveled woman, her face swollen with liquor, came toward us. "Gimme ah . . . ." We thought she was asking for a ride, but we couldn't understand where she wanted to go.

Dobosz, uranium miner
rch Rock, New Mexico, 6/13/79

Many Indian leaders, determined not to be done in by their despair-filled history, feel the only path to their survival depends on economic power: their ability to manage their own resources and to create reservation jobs. Certainly the best example we saw was the Fort Apache Timber Company, owned and operated by the White Mountain Apache Tribe. A mill and logging operation less than one mile from the convenience store, the timber company cuts and sells 110 million board feet a year. To start the company in 1961 the White Mountain Apaches borrowed two million dollars from the Bureau of Indian Affairs, that hapless arm of the federal government. Within seven years the debt, with interest, was repaid. Ever since, the timber company has been highly successful because of both good management and skilled labor.

✻ ✻ ✻

Las Vegas, New Mexico, is an hour's drive around the southern edge of the Sangre de Cristo Mountains from Santa Fe. In the 1920s and 30s, while Santa Fe grew as an artists' and writers' colony, Las Vegas depended on dry-land farming and ranching. During the Depression the town struggled to maintain itself. The town square, once an oasis of tall live oak trees surrounded by two-story brick buildings, took on the shabby appearance of a place where opportunity would knock only once.

Today, Las Vegas exists to support the political agencies of New Mexico's San Miguel County. It is also the home of the state mental hospital. Founded in the 1940s, the hospital is a complex of red-brick buildings, all having the institutional look of the period. Many of the patients are Hispanic and come from isolated, rural communities in New Mexico. We photographed them in the spring of 1980 during Holy Week. Snow was still on the ground. Daily temperatures varied from thirty-five to fifty degrees Fahrenheit, making it too cold to photograph outside. We set up the camera and the white paper in the main cafeteria, facing the morning light flooding in from a wall of windows. At 11:45 A.M., men and women filed in and took trays of food to tables where they sat together. Members of the hospital staff helped them select foods and relax and talk to one another. A woman entered the cafeteria, taking three steps at a time, then stopping until she counted from one to ten. She was in her mid-thirties and wore a white blouse and blue pantsuit. No one interfered with her, but the time she spent to take such precise steps used up most of her lunch period. Avedon asked if he might take a picture of her. She wore, for the portrait, a silver rosary around her neck. After the sitting, she sat and talked with us, quietly. The assistants took several Polaroids to give to her. Avedon handed her the most flattering one. She asked to see the others, and looked carefully at each picture. "Does this look like me?" She held out a close-up of just her face, distorted and blurred by the automatic focus of the Polaroid. "This is the best one of me," she said. "It's how I feel."

✳ ✳ ✳

In a tattoo parlor in San Antonio, Texas, the owner talked about his clients. He told us, "This is a military town, so we're busiest on weekends, and we're jammed on Saturday afternoons." He described the different kinds of tattoos, and talked about the one of which he was most proud: "I like this Mythical Man that I do. His arms are raised. There are wings on his back and a big sunburst behind him with rays coming out of the sun. I need plenty of room. Any guy I sew it on has to have a real big back." By chance, a policeman on his morning beat stopped and joined the conversation. He said we were wasting our time at the parlor. The best tattoos, the real tattoo artists, were in the Bexar County Jail. The owner of the tattoo parlor didn't say anything. We decided to take the policeman's advice and went that morning to the jail. There the prisoners told us how they worked freehand on each other. They drew with sewing needles and stained their punctured skin with Magic Markers. The inmates, mostly Hispanic, liked religious tattoos, especially the Virgin of Guadalupe and Christ's Sorrowful Head. These were often combined with erotic, even pornographic images. All the prisoners were dressed in white uniforms. Avedon photographed on the exercise roof of the jail building. Nearby a group of six prisoners took turns on the basketball court, sinking layup after layup.

✳ ✳ ✳

The Johnson sisters, Loudilla, Loretta, and Kay, live on a wheat farm near Wildhorse, Colorado. They are all in their forties. When she was twenty-one, Loudilla Johnson heard

"I'm a Honky-Tonk Girl," the first song Loretta Lynn ever recorded. "She grabbed my attention; there weren't a lot of girl singers in country music in those days." Loudilla convinced her two sisters to organize a national fan club. "We've been co-presidents of the Loretta Lynn Fan Club for twenty-two years."

The Johnson sisters fix their hair, put on their makeup, and choose their clothes just as Loretta Lynn does. They give the impression of being triplets. They share the same royal blue bedroom they had as young girls. They sleep in three identical beds covered with blue, antique-satin bedspreads. And across from these beds are individual dressing tables with three-way makeup mirrors. The sisters stay up to date with the latest makeup styles by subscribing to *Glamour, Self, Star, Rolling Stone,* and forty-eight other magazines each month. Underneath their dressing-table stools are small drawers where they keep their nylon hose and jewelry. "We feel like sisters with Loretta," says Kay. Each cares about her personal appearance just as the Country-Western star does. When they walk into the wheat fields to help with the harvest they wear "full makeup."

The Johnson sisters are not married and they have never been engaged. "As a trio, we get a lot of strength from each other," Loretta said. "I know without a doubt, I've got Lou and Kay on my side. They are like a continuation of me." Loudilla told a reporter, "A lot of women don't feel complete unless they're married and have children. Well, God has already finished me. I was complete in the beginning." Never has one of the sisters left the farm to start a life of her own. "It would take the heart out of me if one of us left," said Loudilla.

The Johnson sisters keep in touch with fan club members through newsletters mailed from Wildhorse. The letters are packed with information about concert dates, the latest record release, Loretta Lynn's husband, "Mooney," their six children, her Crisco contract. At the end of every newsletter is the call to colors from the Johnson sisters: "Meanwhile remember . . . DO SOMETHING FOR LORETTA EVERY DAY."

From Wildhorse we drove north through Wyoming and into Montana. We passed mile after mile of wheat, ripe and ready for cutting. Custom combines were arriving from as far away as Texas to begin the annual harvest. We stopped in Brockway, a remote town in eastern Montana, where for thirty-three years families and friends have gathered for a rodeo. From a hillside overlooking a small arena, they watched amateur bucking horse events interspersed with children's pony races and a greased pig contest. No one minded that the day was hot and dry and dusty.

The rodeo ended at dusk. Afterwards, we walked over to the Methodist Church for a community supper, then on to the Iron-J Bar and Dancehall. The bar was packed. We watched the best cowboy dancing we had ever seen. Boys who had been on bucking horses that afternoon now had a girl to swing. An old man two-stepped across the floor with a little girl on his hip. All the men, young and old, were great dancers; the women did their best to hold on. One cowboy, without any partner, grabbed a chair, straddled it backwards, and bucked and danced the chair around the hall.

The next day we drove to Jordan, Montana, and met up with the Wheatcroft brothers, Richard and Brad. They drove us south in their pickup, fast, over dusty dirt roads that go like arrows directly from one point to another. Prong-horned antelope darted fitfully from the noise. We never had a casual drive in a pickup. Western drivers are impatient with the endless space.

We stopped to climb a high butte which rose like a sentinel from the flatlands. The Wheatcroft brothers picked up shards of arrowheads, spotting them the way some people can sight a meteorite in a star-filled sky. On top of the butte was a drystone column scaled to a man, built by the second group of wanderers into this part of Montana—sheepmen in search of open range. We continued on to Ingomar, population twenty, surrounded by ten thousand square miles of virtually uninhabited rangeland. To the south is a creek that runs into a grazing district of about seventy-seven thousand unfenced acres. One winter, during a chinook in the early 1900s, a teacher and her two children left school for home. But the unpredictable, warm wind was short-lived; sub-zero temperatures returned. They died along the creek, a short distance from their house. Today, local ranchers run Hereford and Black Angus cattle on what has come to be called "The Froze to Death."

As we entered Ingomar, three children ran up the dirt street to hang onto our pickup. The Wheatcroft brothers took their "hardware" (a model .66 Smith and Wesson, a Colt New Frontier .45, and a .22/.32 Kit gun) off the dashboard and stowed it under the front seat.

We stopped at the Jersey Lily, where a couple of men were drinking at the bar, two teenage boys played pool, and a Japanese man from the seismograph crew of an oil exploration company looked very much alone. We ordered steaks and "Jersey Lily Beans," acknowledged as the best pinto beans in eastern Montana. As we ate, Brad Wheatcroft reminisced. Their grandfather had come to Montana with a wave of homesteaders in 1913 and received

320 semi-arid acres, free, from the United States government. As homesteads were abandoned during droughts and the Depression, the grandfather bought neighboring sections of land for twenty-five cents an acre. Brad and Richard's father took over in the 1950s and ranched the accumulated nine thousand acres. But the margin of profit with cattle was so slim that Brad and two other brothers were forced to look for work off the ranch. In 1978, their father was crushed to death in a tractor accident. Richard, the youngest brother, found him. The responsibility of maintaining the ranch went to Richard. He had no choice.

Montana does not yield easy ways to make a living. In the cattle business, even in a good year, Richard can only hope to hold what the Wheatcrofts already own. Brad said that if they can just hang on a few more years, with all the energy exploration, maybe they will come into some money. "Who knows," he smiled, "we might wind up as the Cabots and the Lodges of Montana."

✻ ✻ ✻

We saw firsthand the single biggest change taking place in the American West since the closing of the open range and the building of the railroads: the energy boom. In the 1970s, the worldwide shortage of crude oil had caused prices to surge, and drilling for domestic oil became more profitable than ever before. New demands forced technological breakthroughs. From the upper reaches of the Williston basin in North Dakota to the Austin Chalk in central Texas, new fields were discovered. Men were needed. Energy companies were taking another look at out-of-fashion fuels like coal. Huge strip-mining operations scraped coal from surface deposits in Wyoming, Montana, and Colorado. Old tunnel mines were reopened; men went back in and dug deeper. Forecasters said coal would make the United States "energy self-sufficient."

The Stansbury Coal Mine in Reliance, Wyoming, was reopened in 1975 after having been shut for almost two decades. The workers were young, rough, and itinerant. They went underground cramped in small vehicles called "mantrips," scratched with graffiti on the doors, seats, and roofs. After fifty feet, daylight disappeared. The "mantrip" continued down to a depth of thirty-five hundred feet. There, in complete darkness, the miners began their long walk to the "face," the seam where coal was being cut. Their commute lasted almost an hour, one way. The men walked through "entry" tunnels no higher than five feet in many places. They walked bent over on rocky, uneven footing; water seeped in from side walls. For us, unaccustomed to the depth and blackness and cramped passageways, all visual bearings were lost; the light from the miners' helmets did little good. We couldn't see. So we strained to hear, and the soundlessness of the tunnels was forbidding. The air was fouled by coal dust, filling our nostrils and throats, covering our faces and clothes. The miners checked the oxygen in the air each hour. In old, worked-out areas of the mine, the "entries" did not always get enough air. This lack of oxygen is as deadly as a poisonous gas. The miners call it "black damp."

There are other dangers in tunnel coal mining: "float dust," for example, tiny particles of coal that accumulate as the cutting machine works at the face of the coal-seam. Just a random spark from the cutting bit can ignite these particles, causing an explosion with the power of dynamite. "Bounce"—a deceptively light-hearted term used by miners to describe the tremendous heave caused by the earth settling—can start a cave-in from which no one escapes.

The young miners like the challenge and the danger. They have discounted the odds of "knowing that some day you might buy it." A miner said, matter-of-factly, "It's not boring. I guess the danger has something to do with it." A face boss told us, "Miners aren't loyal to the company, they're loyal to the coal. They're like sailors going to sea. They pit themselves against the earth the way sailors go out to sea."

And then there are what one mine foreman called the "tender ones," the men who grew up together, went to school together, whose brothers or fathers or uncles are miners, and who, right out of high school, could make top wages in mining. They like working together, working on a team, watching out for each other. Roger Tims, a twenty-one-year-old miner from Reliance, Wyoming, said, "I like it. I really like it down there. Nobody can get to you."

In 1979, when Avedon first photographed in Oklahoma and Texas, the cocksure "gimme cap" had all but replaced the venerable Stetson. Roughnecks and roustabouts swarmed into the oil fields. A West Texas rancher complained, "I have a hard time keeping young cowboys. They can make more money in the oil patch." Traditionally the men working on a drilling rig are tough and idiosyncractic. They work as a team, doing a dangerous job in the "sorriest conditions you ever saw: 110 degrees out in Odessa or minus 40 up on the side of some mountain in Wyoming. It's miserable." But the conditions bind the men together; they know that they can do well what other men cannot do at all.

Drilling for oil is about pressure. A rig worth as much as ten million dollars is run by a crew of five or six men. Three "floorhands" work on the platform joining thirty-foot sections of steel pipe. A "driller" tends the enormous motors that power the rig. And a lone man stands in the derrick ninety feet above the platform, "stabbing" sections of drill pipe in the hole. These men know that more can go wrong than right. As they drill down into the earth through layers of rock, they can hit a pocket of gas at any depth and at any time. The pressure forcing the gas and oil and rocks up the drill pipe causes a friction so great that the gas stream ignites. Within seconds the fire is "hot enough to melt that rig on down like a candle." A "blowout" can last a day or a week or a year.

In 1979, the use of seismic techniques to locate oil trapped in the fractured limestone of the Austin Chalk, forty miles east of the state capital, sparked a full-fledged Texas oil boom. The quiet, agricultural community of Giddings was transformed into the business and residential center of the Austin Chalk formation. "Courthouse boys" and "leasehounds," "roughnecks" and "pipe liners" descended on Giddings, jolting the county seat with new money, land deals, and oil field production. Within a year and a half, over two hundred drilling rigs were running twenty-four hours a day, seven days a week. Living quarters were so scarce that one entrepreneur turned steel oil-storage tanks, ten feet in diameter, on their sides, cut a door in one end with a blow torch, put two bunks and an air conditioner inside, and rented the oil tank-condos for five hundred dollars a month. Mineral rights, the ownership of oil and gas deposits beneath the land's surface, rose from five dollars an acre to five hundred dollars an acre. Some farmers who had once made six thousand dollars a year selling cows now cashed royalty checks totalling eighty thousand dollars a year. The church-going, family-oriented community saw the divorce rate skyrocket.

But the Austin Chalk boom was too good to last; the town of Giddings became the victim of market forces far beyond its conrol. The price per barrel of oil dropped from a high of forty dollars in 1980 to twenty-nine dollars by mid-1982; simultaneously, oil demand fell by fifty percent. The rig count in the Giddings area went below twenty. Oil-field workers drifted to unskilled jobs in other parts of the country. Less than four years after the boom began, the laundromats were almost empty, the spec-house builders found that their bankers' attitudes had changed, and Giddings unwillingly readjusted to the end of over-night success.

In Omaha, Nebraska, and Amarillo, Texas, Avedon again photographed men whose faces were covered—this time in red and purple. They work in meatpacking plants, slaughtering about three hundred head of cattle per hour. With rotating shifts of 100 to 140 men, the plants are in operation 14 to 18 hours a day. The cattle are driven from outside pens up a ramp to a narrow retainer. There, lunging and bawling, each animal is killed by a "knocking gun," which shoots a pin into its head. Immediately a shackle pin, wrapped around the animal's hind leg, jerks it into the air. The carcasses clatter along a rail in front of an assembly line of workers. First a great automatic scythe rips off the hide. Then a man on the "kill floor" splits the animal, cutting off its forelegs and its head, gutting its stomach. The kill floor is loud, hot, and steamy. Hose-water blasts the carcasses, washes the floor, and cleans the blood from the men's chests and arms.

Of all the jobs we saw—in the oil fields, in underground mines, on construction sites—the work in the slaughterhouse was the most exhausting and unrelieved. The odor is sickening, and the noise never lets up.

✥ ✥ ✥

On August 22, 1980, we were eating breakfast at Keith's Lunch and Breakfast in Provo, Utah. A man sat facing us, two booths away. He was gaunt and dirty. He gestured, rolled his eyes, crying as he talked to himself. It was difficult to tell his age. He looked different than the local people in the booths around him. We wondered how to approach him. But when Avedon introduced himself, the man was glad to talk.

His name was Richard Garber. Months before, he had come up from the south to look for work in Utah. He talked about losing his car. It had been impounded for a parking violation and he had no money to get it back. His life was painful, he said, and he wanted to die. He went up into the mountains, alone, for four weeks. He had no food. Once he heard the whine of a train whistle as it snaked along the Utah Valley. He hated the sound. "A train whistle is the loneliest sound you'll ever hear."

Just that morning Garber had walked down from the mountains. He had tried to telephone his mother in a distant state but was told she had been put in a mental institution. He was standing on the corner of Center Street, next to the post office, when a man gave him some money for breakfast at Keith's.

The assistants set up the camera at the end of the parking lot. The light had not yet come over the buildings. In the shadows, the morning air was cold. Avedon talked to Richard Garber during the sitting. He asked him how he felt when he was alone up in the mountains. He continued to photograph as Garber remembered wanting to die. In front of the white seamless paper, in the shade, with only a thin jacket over his "Mardi Gras" T-shirt, he shivered. When the session was over, Avedon stood him in the sunlight.

Later that morning, Richard Garber was taken to the Alcoholic Rehabilitation Center on the outskirts of town. Ironically, alcohol was not one of Garber's problems, but the Center was Provo's only shelter. That afternoon we stopped by to visit him. His spirits had picked up considerably after hourly doses of vitamins and orange juice. He asked us to sit outside on the grass in the sun. We were at an altitude of five thousand feet, looking over Provo and the Utah Valley; the air was cool and dry. Richard Garber continued his story. He was up in the mountains: "All I thought about was Big Macs, French fries, and watermelon." He talked about the kind of work he liked to do. He said he wanted to go to Salt Lake City to be a waiter, not a busboy.

Finally, when we got up to leave and walked towards our car, he stood in the doorway of the Alcoholic Rehabilitation Center. He looked cheerful, he looked as if he might enjoy Salt Lake City. He waved and called out, "'Oh rev wah' or whatever they say."

✫ ✫ ✫

Ten Sleep, Wyoming. Two Dot, Montana. Faith, South Dakota. Jackpot and Winnemucca. Crownpoint and Window Rock. Wolf Creek, Rocksprings, Shiprock and Showlow. One hundred and eighty-nine cities and towns in all. Seventeen states. Seven hundred and fifty-two people photographed. The first portrait was taken on March 10, 1979, in Sweetwater, Texas. The last—October 28, 1984, at the State Fair of Texas.

Laura Wilson

Wilbur Powell, rancher
Ennis, Montana, 7/4/78

ACKNOWLEDGMENTS

ARIZONA

Abbott Sekaquaptewa, CHAIRMAN, HOPI TRIBE
Eugene Sekaquaptewa, ADVISOR, HOPI RESEARCH AND DEVELOPMENT COMPANY
Dr. Robert Matoon, DIRECTOR, LATIN AMERICAN STUDIES; UNIVERSITY OF ARIZONA
Robert W. Baber, PERSONNEL MANAGER, NORANDA LAKESHORE COPPER MINE
Hal Butler, MANAGER, FORT APACHE TIMBER COMPANY
Louise L. Serpa, PHOTOGRAPHER
Johnny Descheny, NAVAJO ADVISOR
Wilson Hunter, Jr., NAVAJO GUIDE
Dr. Robert Breunig, CURATOR, MUSEUM OF NORTHERN ARIZONA

CALIFORNIA

Dr. Norman Gary, CHAIRMAN, DEPARTMENT OF ENTOMOLOGY; UNIVERSITY OF CALIFORNIA

COLORADO

Cathy Geddes, MANAGER, PUBLIC RELATIONS, COLORADO WESTMORELAND, INC.
Lloyd Miller, MINE SUPERINTENDENT, SOMERSET COAL MINE
Al Perry, SALES MANAGER, WESTERN SLOPE CARBON
Tony Durando, GENERAL MANAGER, HAWKNEST COAL MINE
David Scott, COAL MINING ENGINEER, and Anne Scott
Virginia Honeycutt, RODEO PRODUCER
Chris Jouflas, SHEEP RANCHER
Nancy Wood, JOURNALIST
Mel Harmon, MANAGER, PUBLIC RELATIONS, CF&I STEEL CORPORATION

IDAHO

Justin Rice, CHAIRMAN, COEUR D'ALENE MINES CORPORATION
Harry Magnuson, PRESIDENT, SILVER DOLLAR MINING CORPORATION
David Ritchy, EXECUTIVE, COEUR D'ALENE MINES CORPORATION
Mike Sweet, LAWYER
Richard Hart, DIRECTOR, INSTITUTE OF THE AMERICAN WEST

KANSAS

Jennie Chinn, FOLKLORIST, KANSAS FOLKLIFE PROJECT
Larry Hendrix, DIRECTOR, DEPARTMENT OF AGRICULTURE; GARDEN CITY
Ken Albright, DIRECTOR, DEPARTMENT OF AGRICULTURE; HUTCHINSON

MONTANA

Dr. Ronald Losee, ORTHOPEDIC SURGEON
Olive Losee, FOLKLORIST
Nell Johnson, NURSE
Brad Wheatcroft, LAWYER
Annick Smith, FILMMAKER
June Leiby, TEACHER/ADVISOR, HUTTERITE COLONY
Gary Wunderwald, PHOTOGRAPHER, STATE OF MONTANA
Norman Strung, WRITER
Wes Tibbetts, OWNER, MILES CITY LIVESTOCK CENTER
Edna and Dick Dunning, OWNERS, FAN MOUNTAIN MEAT COMPANY
Bud Cooper, MANAGER, CYPRUS INTERNATIONAL TALC MINE
Tona Freeman Blake, WRITER

NEBRASKA

John M. Shonsey, CHAIRMAN, AMERICAN NATIONAL BANK
Mike Shonsey, DIRECTOR, WESTERN NEBRASKA ARTS COUNCIL
Dale Tinstman, CHAIRMAN OF FINANCE, IOWA BEEF PROCESSORS, INC.
Bob Buscher, PRESIDENT, JOHN ROTH & SON
Lynne Ireland, FOLKLORIST, NEBRASKA STATE HISTORICAL SOCIETY

NEVADA

Robert Laxalt, DIRECTOR, UNIVERSITY OF NEVADA PRESS
David Toll, JOURNALIST
Louie Uriarte, BASQUE ADVISOR

NEW MEXICO

Dr. Marta Weigle, FOLKLORIST
William S. Huey, SECRETARY OF NATURAL RESOURCES, NEW MEXICO, and Mary Huey
Dr. George S. Goldstein, SECRETARY OF HEALTH & ENVIRONMENT, NEW MEXICO
Beth Schaefer, LAWYER, DEPARTMENT OF HEALTH & ENVIRONMENT, NEW MEXICO
Dr. Armin Rembe, ONCOLOGIST, and Penny Rembe
James J. Melfi, PRESIDENT, RESERVE OIL & MINERAL CORPORATION
Frank C. Melfi, EX-VICE-PRESIDENT, RESERVE OIL & MINERALS CORPORATION
Dr. Robert Bergman, PSYCHIATRIST, UNIVERSITY OF NEW MEXICO
Dr. Michael Biernoff, PSYCHIATRIST, INDIAN MEDICAL CENTER AT GALLUP
Michael Gibson, ASSISTANT MANAGER OPERATIONS, KERR-MCGEE CORPORATION
Dr. David Fisher, DIRECTOR, NEW MEXICO STATE HOSPITAL
Rev. C. Roca, S.F., PASTOR, SANTUARIO DE CHIMAYO
Meridel Rubenstein, PHOTOGRAPHER
Dr. Donald M. Kerr, DIRECTOR, LOS ALAMOS NATIONAL LABORATORY

NEW YORK

RICHARD AVEDON STUDIO:
Ruedi Hofmann, STUDIO MANAGER/MASTER PRINTER
Shelley Dowell, EXHIBITION COORDINATOR
PHOTOGRAPHIC ASSISTANTS:
Jim Varriale   Shonna Valeska
Richard Corman   John Edelmann   Junichi Izumi   Kaz Nakamura
Drew Carolan   Paul Chan   David Liittschwager
STUDIO STAFF:
Sebastian Chieco   Penny Cobbs
Bill Bachmann   Verlie Fisher

Norma Stevens, PROJECT ADVISOR
Doon Arbus, WRITER
Charles McGrath, WRITER

HARRY N. ABRAMS, INC., PUBLISHERS:
Paul Gottlieb, PRESIDENT & PUBLISHER
Robert Morton, PROJECT DIRECTOR
Beverly Fazio, EDITOR
Shun Yamamoto, PRODUCTION DIRECTOR

NORTH DAKOTA

Nicholas Vroomin, FOLKLORIST
Doreen Chaky, MANAGING EDITOR, WILLISTON BASIN OIL REPORTER
Robert Caudel, SENIOR VICE-PRESIDENT, BANK OF NORTH DAKOTA

OKLAHOMA

George Nigh, GOVERNOR
Betty Price, DIRECTOR, STATE ARTS COUNCIL
Walt Helmerich III, PRESIDENT, HELMERICH & PAYNE OIL CORPORATION
Cecil Covel, TOOL PUSHER, HELMERICH & PAYNE OIL CORPORATION
John A. Taylor, PRESIDENT, JOHN A. TAYLOR PETROLEUM EXPLORATION
Jerome M. Westheimer, PRESIDENT, VALBEL WEST OIL CORPORATION
Duane Le Norman, AREA SUPERINTENDENT, GETTY OIL CORPORATION

THIS BOOK WAS DESIGNED BY MARVIN ISRAEL AND ELIZABETH AVEDON